Ruth's Wonderful Song

A Story for Kids

Ruth's Wonderful Song

A Story for Kids

By

Peter Jennings

With contributions from

Tom Sandler

Published by

Castle Carrington Publishing

2021

Ruth's Wonderful Song
A Story for Kids

First published in paperback in 2021
Cover Design: Margot Wilson and Peter Jennings
Illustrations: Margot Wilson and Tom Sandler

ISBN: 978-1-990096-15-0 (paperback)

Published in Canada by
Castle Carrington Publishing
www.castlecarringtonpublishing.ca
Victoria BC, Canada

Visit the author at:
peterjennings.me
thewonderfulsong.com
More about the book that reveals Ruth Lowe's life:
untilismileatyou.com

Ruth's Wonderful Song

A Story for Kids

Hi. My name's Tommy.

I want to tell you a story.
It's a true story.
And it's a happy story.

It's about my mom.
Her name was Ruth.

Ruth wrote a wonderful song.

And I'm going to tell you about that in a moment.

2

Ruth was very pretty.

And she was lots of fun.

And she loved playing the piano.

She was really good at playing the piano.

Can you play the piano?

4

5

Now, sometimes, my mom, Ruth, was sad.

Do you know why she was sad?

Well, it was because the man she had married, Harold, had died. He died really suddenly.

Poor Ruth was just 23 years old when this happened.

They'd only been married for one year.

When this happened, Ruth just cried and cried.

Wouldn't you cry too if someone you loved died?

One day, my mom came up with a wonderful idea.

She sat down at her old piano.

And guess what happened?

Can you guess?

Well, here's what happened.

She wrote a song.

7

9

It was a song she said just poured out of her heart.

She called it *I'll Never Smile Again.*

It was a sad song. But it was a wonderful song.

Ruth's Wonderful Song.

Now, back in those days, my mom played piano in an orchestra where it was only girls.

They were called *The Melodears.*

You know what an orchestra is, don't you?

It's a group of people who get together and play their musical instruments all together.

All at the same time.

Like the piano. And saxophones. And trumpets. And violins...

All sorts of different instruments are part of the orchestra.

13

Well, there was another orchestra led by a man named Tommy Dorsey. He played the trombone.

My name's Tommy too.

Want to know why?

My name's Tommy because my mom named me after the famous orchestra leader, Tommy Dorsey.

Because she got to meet him.
And they became friends.

Neat, eh?

Anyway, before they ever met, someone got a copy of Ruth's song, *I'll Never Smile Again*, and they gave it to Tommy Dorsey.

He listened to it.

And he liked it.

In fact, he liked it a lot.

He thought it was a wonderful song.

And it was.

Do you know how much he liked it?

Well, Tommy liked Ruth's song so much that he recorded it with his orchestra in a great big studio.

They made a record of Ruth's wonderful song.

And then, can you guess what happened?

15

17

The song became a huge hit.

People listened to it right around the world.
Millions of people loved this song.

Because it was a wonderful song.

Next thing you know, Ruth won all kinds of prizes for writing the song.

And everybody was talking about it.

Ruth became famous for writing her wonderful song.

And as time went by, she wrote lots more songs.

And suddenly, Ruth, my sad mom became... Ruth, my happy mom.

She loved playing her bright yellow piano and writing more songs.

21

Of course, she wasn't my mom yet.

Because she hadn't married my dad yet.

And, of course, he wasn't my dad yet either, in this story.

But, after a while, my mom, Ruth, decided she wanted to get married again.

And my dad, Nat, wanted to get married too.

Ruth and Nat met.

And they fell in love.

And Ruth and Nat got married.

And then ,they had two sons, my brother, Stephen, and me,
Tommy.

25

You know what?

I'm really proud of my mom for writing that famous song,
I'll Never Smile Again.

People are still listening to it today, more than 80 years after
she wrote it.

Why?

Because it's a wonderful song.

Isn't that amazing?

And I'm so proud of my mom for how she did what she did.

You see, back then, most girls didn't have jobs.

They stayed at home, they had babies and they kept the house going.

They were called *Housewives.*

29

But my mom, Ruth, she worked at a job.

She was called a *Songwriter*.

She wrote songs.

Wonderful songs.

Now, most of the other songwriters were men.

But mom was just as good at playing tunes and writing songs as they were.

So, she just kept playing more tunes on her bright yellow piano and writing more songs.

And she did that really well.

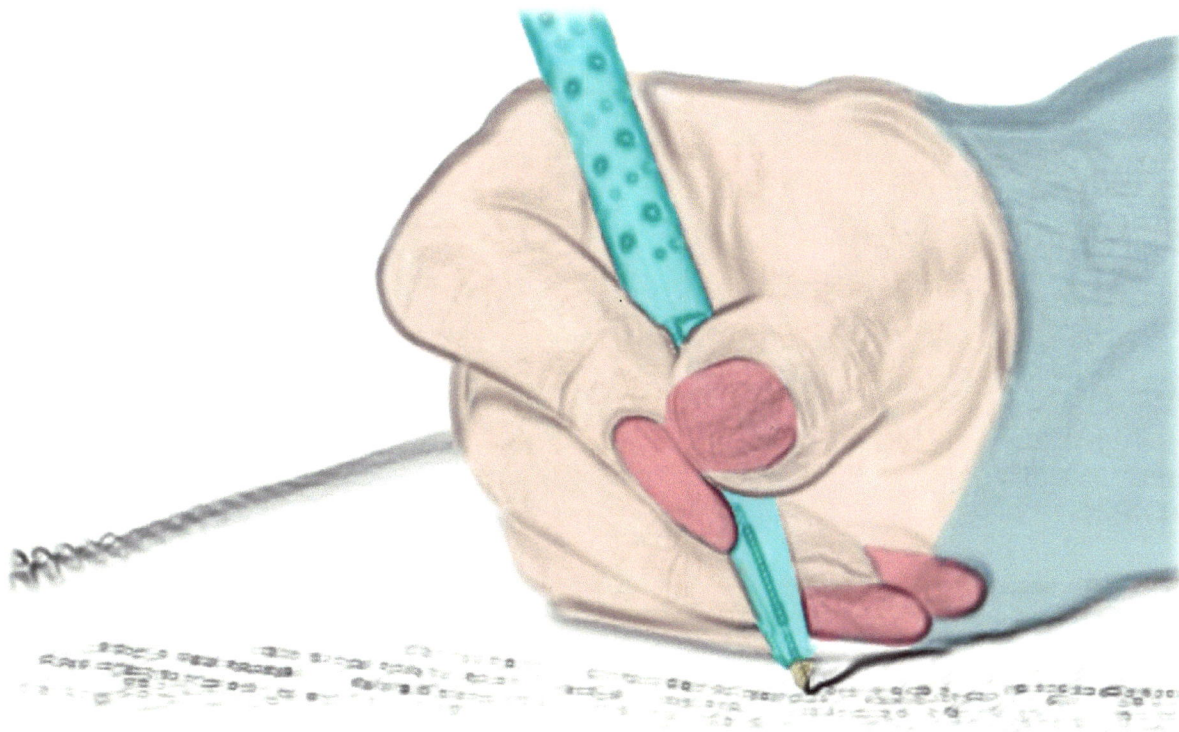

33

As for me, I play the guitar. And I know how to sing.

And I once wrote a song with my mom.

We called it, *Take Your Sins to the River*.
By Ruth and Tommy Sandler.

Maybe I can play it for you sometime.

A few years ago, my mom got sick.
And she died.

That made me sad.
And it still does because I miss her.

But you know what? I'm happy too.

Do you know why I'm happy?

I'm happy because I get to talk about my mom.

I'm happy because I get to tell you how famous Ruth was because of the song that she wrote.

That wonderful song. *I'll Never Smile Again.*

I'm really proud of her.

Thanks for letting me tell you my story about Ruth's wonderful Song.

I'd like to hear your story sometime.

36

www.ingramcontent.com/pod-product-compliance
Lightning Source LLC
LaVergne TN
LVHW072120070426

835511LV00002B/42